My Dearest Hurricane

My Dearest Hurricane

Love and Things that Looked Like It

MORGAN NIKOLA-WREN

Luminarium
PRESS

My Dearest Hurricane

Copyright © 2017 by Morgan Nikola-Wren

ISBN-13: 978-0998589817

ISBN-10:   0998589810

Edited by Julie Guzzetta

To contact the author, email luminariumpress@gmail.com.

for all the loves i've weathered
on my way to where i am

...and especially for the ones
who keep checking to see
if i've written about them.

TABLE OF
CONTENTS

PART 1

The Stirring

I.

all it took
was one touch whispering
against my skin
and i knew
you were going to be
the poems everyone
would ask me about

II.

you look at me
like i may as well know
you're going to wrap yourself
in the deep of me

but i can just as easily crush
as carry you
in the generous swell
of my current

and you
have not yet asked me
which i intend to do

III.

there are futures that seem
so inevitable
they make memories of themselves
far before their time

call it
a second-hand sense
reaching desperate for me
through the music
to graze goosebumps
across my arm

call it
a murky warning
clouding up my ears
just enough to make
your voice a fragrant haze

call it
whatever you like

the point is, i
can see the ghosts
of all we're going to destroy
draped in white wisps
through the air

we're going
to drink each other in
smooth as cigarettes
and twice as deadly
but for now
i just hold your breath hostage
from across the room

IV.

love is
telling me
all the places it hurts the most
and trusting
my words not to wander there
when i think i want
to wound you

and i fear
i am not up
to the challenge

V.

i am a bouquet
of brand new scars
hungry and waiting
to kiss your skin pink and tender

i am ripe, lush fruit—the color
of a bruise in a midnight garden
weighing the trees heavy
with all you're afraid to find in me

VI.

you didn't take
my breath away
my lungs are just learning
from the rest of me

they are wondering if anything
is worth letting in anymore

and i would tell you this
but you keep slipping smiles
into my mouth and they
are crowding out all
the right words

VII.

i think we each know
what a storm–battered soul will do
for a little love

this time, i just want to give
without giving in

to never unlock my kiss for more
than one or two secrets

so let's just get lonely
in each other's arms

VIII.

you've got a smile like a voyage

it starts flecked up in your eyes,
curls round my waist and
pulls me straight into your story
'til i almost forget
what it is that
i am crossing this life in search of
in the first place

i am not one to lose my heart
but if i did,
the first place i would look for it
would be in your hands

IX.

is it you
or your wanting
that is bathing my words in yes?

is it you
or your hunger
that is soaking my skin in sugar?

X.

i've combed my fingers
through each moment,
but i still can't say exactly
when your name stormed its way
into my smile

i've introduced my eyes
to every inch of you
but i still can't tell
where you end
and where the poetry begins

PART 2

The Downpour

I.

these mistakes disguised as me
have tripped over so many stories
to find you

have knotted themselves
through countless arms
just to stain my name
on your skin

so drench my face
in the touch
of your fingers

sweep your whispers through
my ha ir like a wind that is
stirring itself into something
stronger than a single night

II.

dear, you're such a
splendid slice of daring
splashing mischief across my tongue

III.

i kissed you too hard
  our mouths crashing. crushing
    against one another

i inhaled you too deep
  felt you dipping, diving
    your way down
    my throat

i let you build a house
  right inside my ribs,
  and you've been
  hammering my heart
  against my chest ever since

IV.

let's crouch so small into each other
'til this tiny world we've
cornered for ourselves
seems big enough for an escape

let's eat each other alive
just like we promised—
make a banquet
of our shadowy pasts

now, tell me stories, bite–sized boy
set your compass eyes spinning
churning sugar–water words
from a rosebud mouth

i'll peel your secrets off of you
send them fluttering to the ground
like flower petals
like i'll be able to tell if you love me
when there are none left

i will become
all the questions
i am aching to be asked

so bring me
the darkest depths of you
i swear, i won't mind
black was always my color

let's dig through
the trenches of ourselves
and leave love notes
beneath each other's fingernails

V.

here
we are souls set afloat
in a room
adrift with warm trust

here
our lungs let go of
all the shame they have dragged
right up to this moment

here
kinship sails
through our every touch

here
every secret you whisper
against my neck
rests safe in a collarbone cradle

here
you make sense

here
you are safe

here
i will tell you how the story ends
all the possible ways
and you will find me in each of them
waiting right at the spot
where the words run out

VI.

we love each other
in the dark, dizzy-strange ways
that we have yet to teach ourselves

we consume one another
in mouthfuls of promises
that we cannot swallow

VII.

you are every dead end
i ever ran from
and all the love
i am looking for

VIII.

you kiss me
like you left all your best poems
in my mouth

you suggest seeing
how long we can go
speaking only in verse
to each other

you ask
if the words aligning themselves
like stars against my smile
will be so poetic
that they put yours to shame

i tell you
that i save the poetry
for the things i am scared to say

i do not mention
that i could spend years
chasing prose
up the slope of your back

IX.

you've got one of those souls
that ran across centuries
just to jump into your skin

and the sort of voice
that can unbutton me
from my bones

your eyes
glimmer a delicious gold

and my tongue
weeps itself wet

because loving you
means practicing a goodbye
that will smash my teeth to pieces
when it's finally pulled
from my voice

X.

my nerves are awash
in the fantasy of your touch
everything about you is a dream
which is to say
i feel you slip
from my words' reach
every time i try
to explain you to others,
thinning yourself into a haze
until it's clear you have no place
in my reality

PART 8

The Wreckage

I.

you were
my favorite
kind of "almost"

my most beautiful
"not quite"

now,
you're just my secrets
dressed as a stranger

i don't know how
all this unfamiliar landed
on our tongues

how i wound up
cranking out words
slow and stubborn as rust
to someone who used to
catch my secrets in their kiss
before my voice ever had a chance
to find them

II.

your razor tongue
could always cut me
into countless red ribbons
so i tied myself to

       every chair leg

       door handle

       gin bottle

       sink faucet

       hanging lamp

       shower nozzle

       bedpost

       coatrack

       i could find here

so you'd know
i wasn't going anywhere

at least, not 'til i said when

now, this place is a web i
can't work my way out of

III.

for what it's worth
i wanted to want this
to work,
but some names
can't help but sound
like a story you have
no intention of finishing

IV.

we end this
when the starless dark morning
is thick around us
leaning all its indigo close to listen
like it told the whole world
to stay still
to keep the sun tucked in asleep
for just a few moments longer
so it could hear my bid goodbye
to the sinking harbor
of your hands

V.

one of the earth's
most famous cruelties
is how it can just keep turning
no matter what may
have just shattered us

you left and i began counting
the days
until the smell of you would
shake itself free of my clothes
but no matter how long ago
my house emptied itself of
your smile,
i've still got walls full of shadows
trying to shift into the shape of you

VI.

if you just give me
one more chance,
i promise
to tear you apart again
only this time, more gently

VII.

i see you knotted
so tightly into her arms
and the resemblance is striking

it's not just the clothes and hair
it's like you borrowed my smile
without asking
and then gave it to her to wear

VIII.

i knew who you were
from the beginning
and with eyes pulled open,
i asked you to pleasure me blind

now, you look like every other
heartbreak i've heard echoing
through empty coffee cups
across my table,
clouding up the milky eyes
of all the people i've been
called to comfort

i don't know why i thought we
were so special

IX.

i am still trying
to regret you

X.

you always kept a supply
of tinned affection stacked
along the shelves of your aching ribs
for the days when you were dying
to feed on love

and i was
just the nearest mouth
to open wide
to try the words on
and tell you how they tasted

your fingers fumbled for mine
like you had forgotten to feel
your way forward
through the darkness

and when i couldn't
love the lonely out of you
(no one can)
you weighed me
heavy with your heartache,
then grew angry
when you found me
anchored in your arms

XI.

this does not feel
like healing to me

it's flooding the house
with tears and
calling it an ocean
because i want to wash up
anywhere but here

it's building a raft
of kitchen chairs
then acting surprised
when i find myself
wrecked against my bed
each morning

i want nothing more
than to stop drowning
in the smell of your skin

XII.

i always loved how
you could place a night
in my hands and i
would find forever
wrapped inside of it

i mourn for the mess
of memories i've forgotten
while scrubbing you from my mind
so i let some of your words stay
and wrap themselves around me
when my rage has gone to sleep

XIII.

you doused your voice
in denial, but your eyes
were steeped in tears when
you touched me

so, i guess some secrets
will just have to stay between
your hands and i

just know
the next woman's name
and all the others after it
will never stop tasting
like my smile

PART 4

The Repair

I.

most people prefer
to call it "compromise,"
but you can only give up so many
pieces of yourself
before you become
small

II.

i am
searching my spirit
for surviving embers

i cast
dreary skeletal sentences
over and over
into the empty before me,
the swelling tide
of my sighing chest
sinking lower with every
sound i make

i am
swimming across
countless clumsy words
trying to tell myself that i
am a storm of silent fire

in the end
we called it
a sham
a distraction
not the real thing
but like the very best
of lies, our love
had a bit of truth mixed into it

III.

i wonder
if any of my hair
remembers playing in your hands
or if this is the first part of me
to outgrow you

i measure its
timeline crawl down my neck
pull it taut as violin strings
to remind myself that there
is music to be made
whether you are here or not

IV.

we always walked
with my hand
swallowed in yours

everything about you
had tongues

but i am teeth,
my darling boy,
teeth and more starlight
than you could ever
hope to stomach

V.

at least, when people are broken
into this many pieces
they can put themselves
back together
in any shape they like

so i will sculpt myself
into all the words
i wish someone would tell me:

> *my love, forgive yourself*
> *tuck your heart into*
> *your most terrible mistakes*
> *every night*
> *'til you can finally learn*
> *to sleep with what you've done*

befriend your regrets
'til you must call them
by a more comfortable name

i know
i know you are frightened
and it will never be
as easy as you hope
but you'll find it is rarely
as hard as you fear

VI.

in the end i traded us in
for words

not perfect words, mind you
and not many
but enough
enough to lay maps
across the insides of my eyelids

enough to tell me how
to escape into my own arms
when the next disappointment
wrapped in "could be"
comes my way

VII.

it wasn't
all your fault, you know

i fall
just a little
in love with anything
that makes me feel
uncharted and wild

a few springs ago,
it was you

tonight,
it is the stillness
of a city that feels safe enough
to sleep all around me
and the way it tucks starlight
into all my thoughts,
the ones that would have
drowned in the daylight

i want
to take this night by the hand
and run from the sunrise
'til we've walked
the whole world over
together

VIII.

these are such beautiful
hearts we all have
so, let's try to use them
for something other than
breaking

i say we
pour all of our pain
under the floorboards
and stand a bit taller
for doing so

IX.

tonight, the wind
is howling and hell–bent
on strangling me with my own hair

the clouds are fevered
with the lightning they
fling down at me
for the way i shine my grin
up at the thunder

tonight, the rain
cuts down my face
where it thinks tears ought to be

but still, i smile all the same
i hang a war cry across
my throat like a banner as i
shake the universe by the shoulders
'til it gives me the joy i came for
falling in wayward stars from its fists

and i look up for all of it
my chin turned
a defiant kind of skyward
'til the gleam lands back in my eye
where it belongs

Acknowledgements

As always, infinite thanks to God, for sticking around through everything and cosmically blowing away my expectations of Him in a regular basis.

To my friends and family, thank you for tolerating my copious bouts of introversion and my incessant rambling about books when I finally did come out to socialize.

Thank you, Robert, for the awesome journals, and for keeping me full of coffee and good tea. And for thinking I'm even better looking with all my hair cut off.

To my editor, Julie Guzzetta, for taking such good care of my book-children. I'm starting to think of you as that awesome relative that kids go to visit in middle grade novels, coming back with a better sense of who they are and what they want to say.

To Amanda Lovelace and Alison Malee. Thank you for pouring so much care and beauty into your own art, for taking the time to read this work, and for being so enthusiastic about it. That seriously kept me excited about this project when I worried I had nothing to say. I still cannot believe I get each of your beautiful words on this cover!

To The Graphics Fairy, for the cover image, and for finding so many gorgeous, vintage pictures that speak to my steampunk soul.

And to you. Yes, you, with the book in your hands. I'd be writing regardless of pretty much anything, but I'm a writer because of you. Because I keep scribbling out my thoughts and people keep being wonderful about it. I hope something in these pages felt familiar, I hope you know you're not alone, and I hope to be able to thank you personally one day. But in case that doesn't happen, I want you to know you've made such a difference in my life, and I am so grateful for you.

Love, Morgan

66829502R00051

Made in the USA
Lexington, KY
25 August 2017